CROWN CLASSICS

ELIZABETH BARRETT BROWNING

SELECTED POEMS

CROWN CLASSICS

Elizabeth Barrett Browning

Selected Poems

*Selected and introduced by
Anthony Eyre*

MOUNT ORLEANS
PRESS

Crown Classics Poetry Series
Series editor: Louise Guinness

This collection first published in 2019 by
Mount Orleans Press
23 High Street, Cricklade SN6 6AP
https://anthonyeyre.com

CIP data for this title are available from the British Library

Typography and book production by Anthony Eyre

ISBN 978-1-912945-05-4

Printed in Italy
by Esperia, Lavis (TN)

Frontispiece: Elizabeth Barrett Browning,
by Elliott & Fry, after Macaire.
Albumen *carte-de-visite*, September 1858.
© *National Portrait Gallery, London*

CONTENTS

The Cry of the Children   11

The Runaway Slave at Pilgrim's Point   16

Catarina to Camoens   24

Sonnets from the Portuguese   29

A Man's Requirements   39

The Lady's Yes   41

Lord Walter's Wife   44

A Musical Instrument   48

Exaggeration   49

The Deserted Garden   50

Human Life's Mystery   54

Inclusions   56

Substitution   56

Died   57

The Sleep   58

The Best Thing in the World   60

The Churchyard   61

My Doves   62

INTRODUCTION

❧

'I AM "LITTLE AND BLACK" like Sappho, *en attendant* the immortality—five feet one high; as the latitude, straight to correspond—eyes of various colours as the sun shines—called blue and black, without being accidentally black and blue—affidavited for grey, sworn at for hazel—and set down by myself (according to my private view in the glass) as dark-green-brown-grounded with brown, and green otherwise; what is called "invisible green" in invisible garden fences. I should be particular to you who are a colourist. Not much nose of any kind; *certes* no superfluity of nose; but to make up for it, a mouth suitable to a large personality—oh, and a very very little voice, to which Cordelia's was a happy medium. Dark hair and complexion. Small face and sundries.'

So Elizabeth Barrett Browning described herself. 'You who are a colourist' refers to the painter Benjamin Haydon, to whom she wrote this letter. The description is revealing for the light it sheds on Browning's character. So much of her story is overshadowed by her ill health and overbearing father, and so much of her poetry intertwines the themes of death with love, that one perhaps needs reminding that she had this light-hearted, witty and playful side to her character.

Elizabeth was born on 6 March 1806 in County Durham. Her parents were Mary Grahame Clarke and

Edward Barrett Moulton Barrett. She was the eldest of a family which was to comprise some twelve children. Both her father's and her mother's families had made fortunes out of the slave trade, with plantations and other business interests in Jamaica. These were significant in that through inheritance Elizabeth had the financial independence that allowed her to escape her dominant father; and they fired her social conscience and led her to fight for emancipation in poems such as *The Runaway Slave at Pilgrim's Point*.

At the age of three Elizabeth's family moved to what was to be her childhood home, Hope End, near the Malvern Hills in Herefordshire. Her father built an extravagant house in the Turkish style there, to be sold 23 years later as a result of financial difficulties. The house and landscape of Hope End were evoked in Elizabeth's epic poem *Aurora Leigh*, published in 1856.

Aurora Leigh was also autobiographical in describing a childhood surrounded by books. She had access to her father's library, but not the freedom of it: novels such as *Tom Jones* were disallowed. Instead she found a route into the classical world through Alexander Pope's translation of the *Illiad*. She was able to share her younger brother Edward's tutor and studied Latin and Greek. Her reading spanned Enlightenment texts by Paine, Voltaire and Rousseau and reached the early feminist writing of Mary Wollstonecraft. As she wrote later 'Books and dreams were what I lived in and domestic life only seemed to buzz gently round, like the bees about the grass'.

And she wrote poetry. 'I was precocious, and used to make rhymes over my bread and milk when I was nearly a baby.' As she described it in *Aurora Leigh*,

> ...I lived, those days,
> And wrote because I lived—unlicensed else:
> My heart beat in my brain...

Her mother built up a large collection of her juvenile poetry, culminating in *The Battle of Marathon*, an epic poem in four books Elizabeth wrote when was twelve. Her father had this privately printed in 1820.

It was in the 1820s that Elizabeth began to be afflicted by some sort of wasting disease which was never properly diagnosed. It could possibly have related to a fall from her pony, it probably had some sort of spinal connection. The upshot was that it caused her to live the life of an invalid: 'I lie all day, and day after day, on the sofa...'. The fortunes of the family declined. Elizabeth's mother Mary died in 1828. Mismanagement of the Jamaican estates caused the sale of Hope End in 1832. In 1838, after an interlude in Sidmouth, the Barretts settled in London at 50 Wimpole Street.

The story of these years was told in the 1934 Hollywood movie *The Barretts of Wimpole Street*. By this time Elizabeth had published *An Essay on Mind, with Other Poems* (1826); *Prometheus Bound, Translated from the Greek of Aeschylus, and Miscellaneous Poems* (1833); and *The Seraphim, and Other Poems* (1838). In 1844 she published another collection, *Poems*, and these came to the attention of Robert Browning. He started corresponding with 'Dear Miss Barrett', writing 'I love your verses with all my heart', and praising their 'fresh strange music, the affluent language, the exquisite pathos and true new brave thought.' An introduction between the two was arranged by Elizabeth's cousin John Kenyon, and Robert and Elizabeth fell in love. Their marriage, in the teeth of Elizabeth's father's opposition (he disinherited her), was more in the nature of an elopement; but they got away, settling in Italy in September 1846.

Sonnets from the Portuguese date from these years. Elizabeth had written them inspired by her love for Robert: they were intensely personal. It was Robert who convinced her to publish them. The title was intentionally misleading, designed to cover the trail and disguise the fact that the Sonnets are actually the outpourings of Elizabeth's love for Robert. 'My little Portuguese' was his nickname for her, 'little and black' as she described herself. Luís de Camoëns was a Portuguese poet famous for his love sonnets, and Elizabeth's poem *Catarina to Camoens* was one of Robert's favourites.

Married life was a liberation from the sofa in the upper room at Wimpole Street. In social terms she was now meeting a wide range of writers, critics and artists: Ruskin, George Sand, Thackeray, Tennyson and Charles Kingsley, to name but a few. In Italy Elizabeth got caught up in the politics of the *Risorgimento*, meeting Mazzini and devoting *Poems Before Congress*, a collection published in 1860, to the cause of Italian unification.

The Brownings had a son, Robert, born in 1849 and nicknamed 'Pen'. However Elizabeth's health, never robust, deteriorated, with lung complications eased by ever-larger doses of laudanum. She died on 29 June 1861 in Robert's arms, and is buried in the English Cemetery in Florence. Her last poem was *A Musical Instrument*.

THE CRY OF THE CHILDREN

DO ye hear the children weeping, O my brothers,
  Ere the sorrow comes with years?
They are leaning their young heads against their mothers
  And that cannot stop their tears.
The young lambs are bleating in the meadows,
  The young birds are chirping in the nest,
The young fawns are playing with the shadows,
  The young flowers are blowing toward the west
But the young, young children, O my brothers,
  They are weeping bitterly!
They are weeping in the playtime of the others,
  In the country of the free.

Do you question the young children in the sorrow,
  Why their tears are falling so?
The old man may weep for his tomorrow
  Which is lost in Long Ago;
The old tree is leafless in the forest,
  The old year is ending in the frost,
The old wound, if stricken, is the sorest,
  The old hope is hardest to be lost.
But the young, young children, O my brothers
  Do you ask them why they stand
Weeping sore before the bosoms of their mothers,
  In our happy Fatherland?

They look up with their pale and sunken faces,
  And their looks are sad to see,
For the man's hoary anguish draws and presses
  Down the cheeks of infancy.
'Your old earth', they say, 'is very dreary;
  Our young feet', they say, 'are very weak!

Few paces have we taken, yet are weary—
    Our grave-rest is very far to seek.
Ask the aged why they weep, and not the children;
    For the outside earth is cold;
And we young ones stand without, in our bewildering,
    And the graves are for the old.'

'True,' say the children, 'it may happen
    That we die before our time;
Little Alice died last year—her grave is shapen
    Like a snowball, in the rime.
We looked into the pit prepared to take her:
    Was no room for any work in the close clay!
From the sleep wherein she lieth none will wake her,
    Crying, "Get up, little Alice! it is day."
If you listen by that grave, in sun and shower,
    With your ear down, little Alice never cries;
Could we see her face, be sure we should not know her,
    For the smile has time for growing in her eyes:
And merry go her moments, lulled and stilled in
    The shroud by the kirk-chime!
It is good when it happens,' say the children,
    'That we die before our time.'

Alas, alas, the children! they are seeking
    Death in life, as best to have;
They are binding up their hearts away from breaking,
    With a cerement from the grave.
Go out, children, from the mine and from the city,
    Sing out, children, as the little thrushes do;
Pluck you handfuls of the meadow cowslips pretty,
    Laugh aloud to feel your fingers let them through!
But they answer, 'Are your cowslips of the meadows
    Like our weeds anear the mine?
Leave us quiet in the dark of the coal-shadows,
    From your pleasures fair and fine!

'For oh,' say the children, 'we are weary,
    And we cannot run or leap;
If we cared for any meadows, it were merely
    To drop down in them and sleep.
Our knees tremble sorely in the stooping,
    We fall upon our faces, trying to go;
And, underneath our heavy eyelids drooping,
    The reddest flower would look as pale as snow;
For, all day, we drag our burden tiring
    Through the coal-dark, under-ground—
Or, all day, we drive the wheels of iron
    In the factories, round and round.

'For all day, the wheels are droning, turning,
    Their wind comes in our faces,—
Till our hearts turn,—our head, with pulses burning,
    And the walls turn in their places:
Turns the sky in the high window blank and reeling
    Turns the long light that drops adown the wall,
Turn the black flies that crawl along the ceiling,
    All are turning, all the day, and we with all.
And all the day, the iron wheels are droning,
    And sometimes we could pray,
"O ye wheels" (breaking out in a mad moaning),
    "Stop! be silent for to-day!"

Aye! be silent! Let them hear each other breathing
    For a moment, mouth to mouth!
Let them touch each other's hands, in a fresh wreathing
    Of their tender human youth!
Let them feel that this cold metallic motion
    Is not all the life God fashions or reveals:
Let them prove their living souls against the notion
    That they live in you, or under you, O wheels!
Still, all day, the iron wheels go onward,
    Grinding life down from its mark;

And the children's souls, which God is calling sunward,
    Spin on blindly in the dark.

Now tell the poor young children, O my brothers,
    To look up to Him and pray;
So the blessed One who blesseth all the others,
    Will bless them another day.
They answer, 'Who is God that He should hear us,
    While the rushing of the iron wheels is stirred?
When we sob aloud, the human creatures near us
    Pass by, hearing not, or answer not a word.
And we hear not (for the wheels in their resounding)
    Strangers speaking at the door:
Is it likely God, with angels singing round Him,
    Hears our weeping any more?

'Two words, indeed, of praying we remember,
    And at midnight's hour of harm,
"'Our Father", looking upward in the chamber,
    We say softly for a charm!
We know no other words, except "Our Father",
    And we think that, in some pause of angels' song,
God may pluck them with the silence sweet to gather,
    And hold both within His right hand which is strong.
"Our Father!" If He heard us, He would surely
    (For they call him good and mild)
Answer, smiling down the steep world very purely,
    "Come and rest with Me, My child."

'But, no!' say the children, weeping faster,
    'He is speechless as a stone;
And they tell us, of His image is the master
    Who commands us to work on.
Go to!' say the children,—'up in Heaven,
Dark, wheel-like, turning clouds are all we find.
Do not mock us; grief had made us unbelieving—

We look up for God, but tears have made us blind.'
Do you hear the children weeping and disproving,
    O my brothers, what ye preach?
For God's possible is taught by His world's loving,
    And the children doubt of each.

And well may the children weep before you,
    They are weary ere they run;
They have never seen the sunshine, nor the glory
    Which is brighter than the sun.
They know the grief of man, without its wisdom;
    They sink in man's despair, without its calm;
Are slaves, without the liberty in Christdom,
    Are martyrs, by the pang without the palm,
Are worn, as if with age, yet unretrievingly
    The harvest of its memories cannot reap,
Are orphans of the earthly love and heavenly,
    Let them weep! let them weep!

They look up, with their pale and sunken faces,
    And their look is dead to see,
For they mind you of their angels in high places,
    With eyes turned on Deity!—
'How long,' they say, 'how long, O cruel nation,
    Will you stand, to move the world, on a child's heart,—
Stifle down with a mailed heel its palpitation,
    And tread onward to your throne amid the mart?
Our blood splashes upward, O gold-heaper,
    And your purple shows your path!
But the child's sob in the silence curses deeper,
    Than the strong man in his wrath.'

THE RUNAWAY SLAVE AT PILGRIM'S POINT

I STAND on the mark beside the shore
Of the first white pilgrim's bended knee,
Where exile turned to ancestor,
And God was thanked for liberty.
I have run through the night, my skin is as dark,
I bend my knee down on this mark...
I look on the sky and the sea.

O pilgrim-souls, I speak to you!
I see you come out proud and slow
From the land of the spirits pale as dew...
And round me and round me ye go!
O pilgrims, I have gasped and run
All night long from the whips of one
Who in your names works sin and woe.

And thus I thought that I would come
And kneel here where I knelt before,
And feel your souls around me hum
In undertone to the ocean's roar;
And lift my black face, my black hand,
Here, in your names, to curse this land
Ye blessed in freedom's evermore.

I am black, I am black;
And yet God made me, they say.
But if He did so, smiling back
He must have cast His work away
Under the feet of His white creatures,
With a look of scorn,—that the dusky features
Might be trodden again to clay.

And yet He has made dark things
To be glad and merry as light.
There's a little dark bird sits and sings;
There's a dark stream ripples out of sight;
And the dark frogs chant in the safe morass,
And the sweetest stars are made to pass
O'er the face of the darkest night.

But we who are dark, we are dark!
Ah, God, we have no stars!
About our souls in care and cark
Our blackness shuts like prison bars:
The poor souls crouch so far behind,
That never a comfort can they find
By reaching through the prison-bars.

Indeed, we live beneath the sky,...
That great smooth Hand of God, stretched out
On all His children fatherly,
To bless them from the fear and doubt,
Which would be, if, from this low place,
All opened straight up to His face
Into the grand eternity.

And still God's sunshine and His frost,
They make us hot, they make us cold,
As if we were not black and lost:
And the beasts and birds, in wood and fold,
Do fear and take us for very men!
Could the weep-poor-will or the cat of the glen
Look into my eyes and be bold?

I am black, I am black!—
But, once, I laughed in girlish glee;
For one of my colour stood in the track
Where the drivers drove, and looked at me—

And tender and full was the look he gave:
Could a slave look so at another slave?—
I look at the sky and the sea.

And from that hour our spirits grew
As free as if unsold, unbought:
Oh, strong enough, since we were two
To conquer the world, we thought!
The drivers drove us day by day;
We did not mind, we went one way,
And no better a liberty sought.

In the sunny ground between the canes,
He said 'I love you' as he passed:
When the shingle-roof rang sharp with the rains,
I heard how he vowed it fast:
While others shook, he smiled in the hut
As he carved me a bowl of the cocoa-nut,
Through the roar of the hurricanes.

I sang his name instead of a song;
Over and over I sang his name—
Upward and downward I drew it along
My various notes; the same, the same!
I sang it low, that the slave-girls near
Might never guess from aught they could hear,
It was only a name.

I look on the sky and the sea—
We were two to love, and two to pray,—
Yes, two, O God, who cried to Thee,
Though nothing didst Thou say.
Coldly Thou sat'st behind the sun!
And now I cry who am but one,
How wilt Thou speak to-day?—

We were black, we were black!
We had no claim to love and bliss:
What marvel, if each turned to lack?
They wrung my cold hands out of his,—
They dragged him... where?... I crawled to touch
His blood's mark in the dust!... not much,
Ye pilgrim-souls,... though plain as this!

Wrong, followed by a deeper wrong!
Mere grief's too good for such as I.
So the white men brought the shame ere long
To strangle the sob of my agony.
They would not leave me for my dull
Wet eyes!—it was too merciful
To let me weep pure tears and die.

I am black, I am black!—
I wore a child upon my breast
An amulet that hung too slack,
And, in my unrest, could not rest:
Thus we went moaning, child and mother,
One to another, one to another,
Until all ended for the best:

For hark ! I will tell you low... low...
I am black, you see,—
And the babe who lay on my bosom so,
Was far too white—too white for me;
As white as the ladies who scorned to pray
Beside me at church but yesterday;
Though my tears had washed a place for my knee.

My own, own child! I could not bear
To look in his face, it was so white.
I covered him up with a kerchief there;
I covered his face in close and tight:

And he moaned and struggled, as well might be,
For the white child wanted his liberty—
Ha, ha! he wanted his master right.

He moaned and beat with his head and feet,
His little feet that never grew—
He struck them out, as it was meet,
Against my heart to break it through.
I might have sung and made him mild—
But I dared not sing to the white-faced child
The only song I knew.

I pulled the kerchief very close:
He could not see the sun, I swear,
More, then, alive, than now he does
From between the roots of the mango... where
...I know where. Close! a child and mother
Do wrong to look at one another,
When one is black and one is fair.

Why, in that single glance I had
Of my child's face,... I tell you all,
I saw a look that made me mad...
The master's look, that used to fall
On my soul like his lash... or worse!
And so, to save it from my curse,
I twisted it round in my shawl.

And he moaned and trembled from foot to head,
He shivered from head to foot;
Till, after a time, he lay instead
Too suddenly still and mute.
I felt, beside, a stiffening cold,...
I dared to lift up just a fold...
As in lifting a leaf of the mango-fruit.

But my fruit... ha, ha!—there, had been
(I laugh to think on't at this hour!...)
Your fine white angels, who have seen
Nearest the secret of God's power,...
And plucked my fruit to make them wine,
And sucked the soul of that child of mine,
As the humming-bird sucks the soul of the flower.

Ha, ha, for the trick of the angels white!
They freed the white child's spirit so.
I said not a word, but, day and night,
I carried the body to and fro;
And it lay on my heart like a stone... as chill.
—The sun may shine out as much as he will:
I am cold, though it happened a month ago.

From the white man's house, and the black man's hut,
I carried the little body on,
The forest's arms did round us shut,
And silence through the trees did run:
They asked no question as I went,—
They stood too high for astonishment,—
They could see God sit on His throne.

My little body, kerchiefed fast,
I bore it on through the forest... on:
And when I felt it was tired at last,
I scooped a hole beneath the moon.
Through the forest-tops the angels far,
With a white sharp finger from every star,
Did point and mock at what was done.

Yet when it was all done aright,...
Earth, 'twixt me and my baby, strewed,
All, changed to black earth,... nothing white,...
A dark child in the dark,—ensued

Some comfort, and my heart grew young:
I sate down smiling there and sung
The song I learnt in my maidenhood.

And thus we two were reconciled,
The white child and black mother, thus:
For, as I sang it, soft and wild
The same song, more melodious,
Rose from the grave whereon I sate!
It was the dead child singing that,
To join the souls of both of us.

I look on the sea and the sky!
Where the pilgrims' ships first anchored lay,
The free sun rideth gloriously;
But the pilgrim-ghosts have slid away
Through the earliest streaks of the morn.
My face is black, but it glares with a scorn
Which they dare not meet by day.

Ah!—in their 'stead, their hunter sons!
Ah, ah! they are on me—they hunt in a ring—
Keep off! I brave you all at once—
I throw off your eyes like snakes that sting!
You have killed the black eagle at nest, I think:
Did you never stand still in your triumph, and shrink
From the stroke of her wounded wing?

(Man, drop that stone you dared to lift!—)
I wish you, who stand there five a-breast,
Each, for his own wife's joy and gift,
A little corpse as safely at rest
As mine in the mangos!—Yes, but she
May keep live babies on her knee,
And sing the song she liketh best.

I am not mad: I am black.
I see you staring in my face—
I know you, staring, shrinking back—
Ye are born of the Washington-race:
And this land is the free America:
And this mark on my wrist… (I prove what I say)
Ropes tied me up here to the flogging-place.

You think I shrieked then? Not a sound!
I hung, as a gourd hangs in the sun.
I only cursed them all around,
As softly as I might have done
My very own child!—From these sands
Up to the mountains, lift your hands,
O slaves, and end what I begun!

Whips, curses; these must answer those!
For in this UNION, you have set
Two kinds of men in adverse rows,
Each loathing each: and all forget
The seven wounds in Christ's body fair;
While HE sees gaping everywhere
Our countless wounds that pay no debt.

Our wounds are different. Your white men
Are, after all, not gods indeed,
Nor able to make Christs again
Do good with bleeding. We who bleed…
(Stand off!) we help not in our loss!
We are too heavy for our cross,
And fall and crush you and your seed.

I fall, I swoon! I look at the sky:
The clouds are breaking on my brain;
I am floated along, as if I should die
Of liberty's exquisite pain—

In the name of the white child, waiting for me
In the death-dark where we may kiss and agree,
White men, I leave you all curse-free
In my broken heart's disdain!

CATARINA TO CAMOENS

ON the door you will not enter
   I have gazed too long: adieu!
Hope withdraws her "peradventure";
   Death is near me,—and not you!
     Come, O lover,
     Close and cover
These poor eyes you called, I ween,
"Sweetest eyes were ever seen!"

When I heard you sing that burden
   In my vernal days and bowers,
Other praises disregarding,
   I but hearkened that of yours,
     Only saying
     In heart-playing,
"Blessèd eyes mine eyes have been,
If the sweetest HIS have seen!"

But all changes. At this vesper
   Cold the sun shines down the door.
If you stood there, would you whisper,
   "Love, I love you," as before,—
     Death pervading
     Now and shading
Eyes you sang of, that yestreen,
As the sweetest ever seen?

Yes, I think, were you beside them,
 Near the bed I die upon,
Though their beauty you denied them,
 As you stood there looking down,
  You would truly
  Call them duly,
For the love's sake found therein,
"Sweetest eyes were ever seen."

And if you looked down upon them,
 And if they looked up to you,
All the light which has foregone them
 Would be gathered back anew;
  They would truly
  Be as duly
Love-transformed to beauty's sheen,
"Sweetest eyes were ever seen."

But, ah me! you only see me,
 In your thoughts of loving man,
Smiling soft, perhaps, and dreamy,
 Through the wavings of my fan;
  And unweeting
  Go repeating
In your revery serene,
"Sweetest eyes were ever seen."

While my spirit leans and reaches
 From my body still and pale,
Fain to hear what tender speech is
 In your love to help my bale.
  O my poet,
  Come and show it!
Come, latest love, to glean
"Sweetest eyes were ever seen."

O my poet, O my prophet!
  When you praised their sweetness so,
Did you think, in singing of it,
  That it might be near to go?
    Had you fancies
    From their glances,
That the grave would quickly screen
"Sweetest eyes were ever seen"?

No reply. The fountain's warble
  In the courtyard sounds alone.
As the water to the marble
  So my heart falls with a moan
    From love-sighing
    To this dying.
Death forerunneth Love to win
"Sweetest eyes were ever seen."

Will you come? When I'm departed
  Where all sweetnesses are hid,
Where thy voice, my tender-hearted,
  Will not lift up either lid,
    Cry, O lover,
    Love is over!
Cry, beneath the cypress green,
"Sweetest eyes were ever seen!"

When the Angelus is ringing,
  Near the convent will you walk,
And recall the choral singing
  Which brought angels down our talk?
    Spirit-shriven
    I viewed heaven,
Till you smiled—"Is earth unclean,
Sweetest eyes were ever seen?"

When beneath the palace-lattice
   You ride slow as you have done,
And you see a face there that is
   Not the old familiar one,
     Will you oftly
     Murmur softly,
"Here ye watched me morn and e'en,
Sweetest eyes were ever seen"?

When the palace-ladies, sitting
   Round your gittern, shall have said,
"Poets, sing those verses written
   For the lady who is dead,"
     Will you tremble,
     Yet dissemble,
Or sing hoarse, with tears between,
"Sweetest eyes were ever seen"?

"Sweetest eyes!" How sweet in flowings
   The repeated cadence is!
Though you sang a hundred poems,
   Still the best one would be this.
     I can hear it
     'Twixt my spirit
And the earth-noise intervene,—
"Sweetest eyes were ever seen!"

But the priest waits for the praying,
   And the choir are on their knees,
And the soul must pass away in
   Strains more solemn-high than these.
     Miserere
     For the weary!
Oh, no longer for Catrine
"Sweetest eyes were ever seen!"

Keep my riband, take and keep it,
  (I have loosed it from my hair)
Feeling, while you overweep it,
   Not alone in your despair,
     Since with saintly
     Watch unfaintly
Out of heaven shall o'er you lean
"Sweetest eyes were ever seen."

But—but now—yet unremovèd
  Up to heaven they glisten fast;
You may cast away, belovèd,
   In your future all my past:
     Such old phrases
     May be praises
For some fairer bosom-queen—
"Sweetest eyes were ever seen!"

Eyes of mine, what are ye doing?
  Faithless, faithless, praised amiss;
If a tear be, on your showing,
   Dropped for any hope of HIS!
     Death has boldness
     Besides coldness,
If unworthy tears demean
"Sweetest eyes were ever seen."

I will look out to his future;
  I will bless it till it shine.
Should he ever be a suitor
   Unto sweeter eyes than mine,
     Sunshine gild them,
     Angels shield them,
Whatsoever eyes terrene
Be the sweetest HIS have seen.

SONNETS FROM THE PORTUGUESE

I

I THOUGHT once how Theocritus had sung
Of the sweet years, the dear and wished-for years,
Who each one in a gracious hand appears
To bear a gift for mortals, old or young:
And, as I mused it in his antique tongue,
I saw, in gradual vision through my tears,
The sweet, sad years, the melancholy years,
Those of my own life, who by turns had flung
A shadow across me. Straightway I was 'ware,
So weeping, how a mystic Shape did move
Behind me, and drew me backward by the hair,
And a voice said in mastery while I strove,...
'Guess now who holds thee?'—'Death,' I said. But there,
The silver answer rang,... 'Not Death, but Love.'

I I

But only three in all God's universe
Have heard this word thou hast said,—Himself, beside
Thee speaking, and me listening! and replied
One of us... that was God,... and laid the curse
So darkly on my eyelids, as to amerce
My sight from seeing thee,—that if I had died,
The deathweights, placed there, would have signified
Less absolute exclusion. 'Nay' is worse
From God than from all others, O my friend!
Men could not part us with their worldly jars,
Nor the seas change us, nor the tempests bend;
Our hands would touch for all the mountain-bars,
And, heaven being rolled between us at the end,
We should but vow the faster for the stars.

VI

Go from me. Yet I feel that I shall stand
Henceforward in thy shadow. Nevermore
Alone upon the threshold of my door
Of individual life, I shall command
The uses of my soul, nor lift my hand
Serenely in the sunshine as before,
Without the sense of that which I forbore,…
Thy touch upon the palm. The widest land
Doom takes to part us, leaves thy heart in mine
With pulses that beat double. What I do
And what I dream include thee, as the wine
Must taste of its own grapes. And when I sue
God for myself, He hears that name of thine,
And sees within my eyes the tears of two.

VII

The face of all the world is changed, I think,
Since first I heard the footsteps of thy soul
Move still, oh, still, beside me, as they stole
Betwixt me and the dreadful outer brink
Of obvious death, where I, who thought to sink,
Was caught up into love, and taught the whole
Of life in a new rhythm. The cup of dole
God gave for baptism, I am fain to drink,
And praise its sweetness, Sweet with thee anear.
The names of country, heaven, are changed away
For where thou art or shalt be, there or here;
And this… this lute and song… loved yesterday
(The singing angels know) are only dear,
Because thy name moves right in what they say.

X

Yet, love, mere love, is beautiful indeed
And worthy of acceptation. Fire is bright,
Let temple burn, or flax. An equal light
Leaps in the flame from cedar-plank or weed.
And love is fire; and when I say at need
I love thee… mark!… I love thee!… in thy sight
I stand transfigured, glorified aright,
With conscience of the new rays that proceed
Out of my face toward thine. There's nothing low
In love, when love the lowest: meanest creatures
Who love God, God accepts while loving so.
And what I feel, across the inferior features
Of what I am, doth flash itself, and show
How that great work of Love enhances Nature's.

XII

Indeed this very love which is my boast,
And which, when rising up from breast to brow,
Doth crown me with a ruby large enow
To draw men's eyes and prove the inner cost,…
This love even, all my worth, to the uttermost,
I should not love withal, unless that thou
Hadst set me an example, shown me how,
When first thine earnest eyes with mine were crossed,
And love called love. And thus, I cannot speak
Of love even, as a good thing of my own.
Thy soul hath snatched up mine all faint and weak,
And placed it by thee on a golden throne,—
And that I love (O soul, we must be meek!)
Is by thee only, whom I love alone.

XIII

And wilt thou have me fashion into speech
The love I bear thee, finding words enough,
And hold the torch out, while the winds are rough,
Between our faces, to cast light on each?—
I drop it at thy feet. I cannot teach
My hand to hold my spirit so far off
From myself... me... that I should bring thee proof
In words, of love hid in me out of reach.
Nay, let the silence of my womanhood
Commend my woman-love to thy belief,—
Seeing that I stand unwon, however wooed,
And rend the garment of my life, in brief,
By a most dauntless, voiceless fortitude,
Lest one touch of this heart convey its grief.

XIV

If thou must love me, let it be for nought
Except for love's sake only. Do not say
'I love her for her smile... her look... her way
Of speaking gently,... for a trick of thought
That falls in well with mine, and certes brought
A sense of pleasant ease on such a day'—
For these things in themselves, Beloved, may
Be changed, or change for thee,—and love, so wrought,
May be unwrought so. Neither love me for
Thine own dear pity's wiping my cheeks dry,—
A creature might forget to weep, who bore
Thy comfort long, and lose thy love thereby!
But love me for love's sake, that evermore
Thou mayst love on, through love's eternity.

X V

Accuse me not, beseech thee, that I wear
Too calm and sad a face in front of thine;
For we two look two ways, and cannot shine
With the same sunlight on our brow and hair.
On me thou lookest, with no doubting care
As on a bee shut in a crystaline,—
Since sorrow hath shut me safe in love's divine,
And to spread wing and fly in the outer air
Were most impossible failure, if I strove
To fail so. But I look on thee... on thee...
Beholding, besides love, the end of love,
Hearing oblivion beyond memory!
As one who sits and gazes from above,
Over the rivers to the bitter sea.

X X

Beloved, my Beloved, when I think
That thou wast in the world a year ago,
What time I sate alone here in the snow
And saw no footprint, heard the silence sink
No moment at thy voice,... but, link by link,
Went counting all my chains, as if that so
They never could fall off at any blow
Struck by thy possible hand... why, thus I drink
Of life's great cup of wonder! Wonderful,
Never to feel thee thrill the day or night
With personal act or speech,—nor even cull
Some prescience of thee with the blossoms white
Thou sawest growing! Atheists are as dull,
Who cannot guess God's presence out of sight.

XXI

Say over again, and yet once over again,
That thou dost love me. Though the word repeated
Should seem 'a cuckoo-song' as thou dost treat it,
Remember, never to the hill or plain,
Valley and wood, without her cuckoo-strain,
Comes the fresh Spring in all her green completed.
Beloved, I, amid the darkness greeted
By a doubtful spirit-voice, in that doubt's pain
Cry…'Speak once more… thou lovest!' Who can fear
Too many stars, though each in heaven shall roll—
Too many flowers, though each shall crown the year?
Say thou dost love me, love me, love me—toll
The silver iterance!—only minding, dear,
To love me also in silence, with thy soul.

XXII

When our two souls stand up erect and strong
Face to face, silent, drawing nigh and nigher,
Until the lengthening wings break into fire
At either curved point,—what bitter wrong
Can the earth do to us, that we should not long
Be here contented? Think. In mounting higher,
The angels would press on us, and aspire
To drop some golden orb of perfect song
Into our deep, dear silence. Let us stay
Rather on earth, Beloved,—where the unfit
Contrarious moods of men recoil away
And isolate pure spirits, and permit
A place to stand and love in for a day,
With darkness and the death-hour rounding it.

XXIII

Is it indeed so? If I lay here dead,
Wouldst thou miss any life in losing mine?
And would the sun for thee more coldly shine,
Because of grave-damps falling round my head?
I marvelled, my Beloved, when I read
Thy thoughts so in the letter. I am thine—
But... so much to thee? Can I pour thy wine
While my hands tremble? Then my soul, instead
Of dreams of death, resumes life's lower range.
Then, love me, Love! look on me... breathe on me!
As brighter ladies do not count it strange,
For love, to give up acres and degree,
I yield the grave for thy sake, and exchange
My near sweet view of Heaven, for earth with thee!

XXVI

I lived with visions for my company,
Instead of men and women, years ago,
And found them gentle mates, nor thought to know
A sweeter music than they played to me.
But soon their trailing purple was not free
Of this world's dust,—their lutes did silent grow,
And I myself grew faint and blind below
Their vanishing eyes. Then *thou* didst come... to be,
Beloved, what they seemed. Their shining fronts,
Their songs, their splendours (better, yet the same,
As river-water hallowed into fonts),
Met in thee, and from out thee overcame
My soul with satisfaction of all wants—
Because God's gifts put man's best dreams to shame.

XXIX

I *think* of thee!—my thoughts do twine and bud
About thee, as wild vines, about a tree,
Put out broad leaves, and soon there's nought to see
Except the straggling green which hides the wood.
Yet, O my palm-tree, be it understood
I will not have my thoughts instead of thee
Who art dearer, better! rather instantly
Renew thy presence. As a strong tree should,
Rustle thy boughs and set thy trunk all bare,
And let these bands of greenery which insphere thee,
Drop heavily down,... burst, shattered, everywhere!
Because, in this deep joy to see and hear thee
And breathe within thy shadow a new air,
I do not think of thee—I am too near thee.

XXXIII

Yes, call me by my pet-name! let me hear
The name I used to run at, when a child
From innocent play, and leave the cowslips piled,
To glance up in some face that proved me dear
With the look of its eyes. I miss the clear
Fond voices, which, being drawn and reconciled
Into the music of Heaven's undefiled,
Call me no longer. Silence on the bier,
While I call God... call God!—so let thy mouth
Be heir to those who are now exanimate.
Gather the north flowers to complete the south,
And catch the early love up in the late.
Yes, call me by that narne,—and I, in truth
With the same heart, will answer, and not wait.

XXXIV

With the same heart, I said, 'I'll answer thee
As those, when thou shalt call me by my name—
Lo, the vain promise! is the same, the same,
Perplexed and ruffled by life's strategy?
When called before, I told how hastily
I dropped my flowers or brake off from a game,
To run and answer with the smile that came
At play last moment, and went on with me
Through my obedience. When I answer now,
I drop a grave thought—break from solitude;
Yet still my heart goes to thee... ponder how...
Not as to a single good, but all my good!
Lay thy hand on it, best one, and allow
That no child's foot would run fast as this blood.

XXXV

If I leave all for thee, wilt thou exchange
And be all to me? Shall I never miss
Home-talk and blessing and the common kiss
That comes to each in turn, nor count it strange
When I look up, to drop on a new range
Of walls and flowers... another home than this?
Nay, wilt thou fill that place by me which is
Filled by dead eyes too tender to know change?
That's hardest. If to conquer love, has tried,
To conquer grief, tries more... as all things prove;
For grief indeed is love and grief beside.
Alas, I have grieved so I am hard to love.
Yet love me—wilt thou? Open thine heart wide,
And fold within, the wet wings of thy dove.

XLIII

How do I love thee? Let me count the ways.
I love thee to the depth and breadth and height
My soul can reach, when feeling out of sight
For the ends of Being and ideal Grace.
I love thee to the level of every day's
Most quiet need, by sun and candlelight.
I love thee freely, as men strive for Right;
I love thee purely, as they turn from Praise.
I love thee with the passion put to use
In my old griefs, and with my childhood's faith.
I love thee with a love I seemed to lose
With my lost saints,—I love thee with the breath,
Smiles, tears, of all my life!—and, if God choose,
I shall but love thee better after death.

XLIV

Beloved thou hast brought me many flowers
Plucked in the garden, all the summer through
And winter, and it seemed as if they grew
In this close room, nor missed the sun and showers.
So, in the like name of that love of ours,
Take back these thoughts which here unfolded too,
And which on warm and cold days I withdrew
From my heart's ground. Indeed, those beds and bowers
Be overgrown with bitter weeds and rue,
And wait thy weeding; yet here's eglantine,
Here's ivy!—take them, as I used to do
Thy flowers, and keep them where they shall not pine.
Instruct thine eyes to keep their colours true,
And tell thy soul, their roots are left in mine.

A MAN'S REQUIREMENTS

LOVE me Sweet, with all thou art,
   Feeling, thinking, seeing;
Love me in the lightest part,
   Love me in full being.

Love me with thine open youth
   In its frank surrender;
With the vowing of thy mouth,
   With its silence tender.

Love me with thine azure eyes,
   Made for earnest granting;
Taking colour from the skies,
   Can Heaven's truth be wanting?

Love me with their lids, that fall
   Snow-like at first meeting;
Love me with thine heart, that all
   Neighbours then see beating.

Love me with thine hand stretched out
   Freely—open-minded:
Love me with thy loitering foot,—
   Hearing one behind it.

Love me with thy voice, that turns
   Sudden faint above me;
Love me with thy blush that burns
   When I murmur *Love me!*

Love me with thy thinking soul,
   Break it to love-sighing;
Love me with thy thoughts that roll
   On through living—dying.

Love me when in thy gorgeous airs,
   When the world has crowned thee;
Love me, kneeling at thy prayers,
   With the angels round thee.

Love me pure, as musers do,
   Up the woodlands shady:
Love me gaily, fast and true
   As a winsome lady.

Through all hopes that keep us brave,
   Farther off or nigher,
Love me for the house and grave,
   And for something higher.

Thus, if thou wilt prove me, Dear,
   Woman's love no fable.
I will love *thee*—half a year—
   As a man is able.

THE LADY'S YES

"YES!" I answered you last night;
"No!" this morning, Sir, I say!
Colours, seen by candle-light,
Will not look the same by day.

When the tabors played their best,
Lamps above, and laughs below—
Love me sounded like a jest,
Fit for *Yes* or fit for *No!*

Call me false, or call me free—
Vow, whatever light may shine,
No man on your face shall see
Any grief for change on mine.

Yet the sin is on us both—
Time to dance is not to woo—
Wooer light makes fickle troth—
Scorn of *me* recoils on *you!*

Learn to win a lady's faith
Nobly, as the thing is high;
Bravely, as for life and death—
With a loyal gravity.

Lead her from the festive boards,
Point her to the starry skies,
Guard her, by your truthful words,
Pure from courtship's flatteries.

By your truth she shall be true—
Ever true, as wives of yore—
And her *Yes*, once said to you,
SHALL be Yes for evermore.

PROOF AND DISPROOF

DOST thou love me, my beloved?
　　Who shall answer yes or no?
What is provèd or disprovèd
　　When my soul inquireth so,
Dost thou love me, my beloved?

I have seen thy heart to-day,
　　Never open to the crowd,
While to love me ay and ay
　　Was the vow as it was vowed
By thine eyes of steadfast grey.

Now I sit alone, alone—
　　And the hot tears break and burn.
Now, Beloved, thou art gone,
　　Doubt and terror have their turn.
Is it love that I have known.

I have known some bitter things,—
　　Anguish, anger, solitude.
Year by year an evil brings,
　　Year by year denies a good;
March winds violate my springs.

I have known how sickness bends,
　　I have known how sorrow breaks,—
How quick hopes have sudden ends,
　　How the heart thinks till it aches
Of the smile of buried friends.

Last, I have known thee, my brave
   Noble thinker, lover, doer!
The best knowledge last I have
   But thou earnest as the thrower
Of fresh flowers upon a grave.

Count what feelings used to move me!
   Can this love assort with those?
Thou, who art so far above me,
   Wilt thou stoop so, for repose?
Is it true that thou canst love me?

Do not blame me if I doubt thee.
   I can call love by its name
When thine arm is wrapt about me;
   But even love seems not the same,
When I sit alone without thee.

In thy clear eyes I descried
   Many a proof of love, to-day;
But tonight, those unbelied
   Speechful eyes being gone away,
There's the proof to seek, beside.

Dost thou love me, my beloved?
   Only thou canst answer yes!
And, thou gone, the proof's disproved,
   And the cry rings answerless—
Dost thou love me, my beloved?

LORD WALTER'S WIFE

'But where do you go?' said the lady,
  While both sat under the yew,
And her eyes were alive in their depth,
  As the kraken beneath the sea-blue.

'Because I fear you,' he answered;—
  'Because you are far too fair,
And able to strangle my soul
  In a mesh of your gold-coloured hair.'

'Oh that,' she said, 'is no reason!
  Such knots are quickly undone,
And too much beauty, I reckon,
  Is nothing but too much sun.'

'Yet farewell so,' he answered;—
  'The sunstroke's fatal at times.
I value your husband, Lord Walter,
  Whose gallop rings still from the limes.'

'Oh that,' she said, 'is no reason.
  You smell a rose through a fence:
If two should smell it what matter?
  Who grumbles, and where's the pretense?'

'But I,' he replied, 'have promised another,
  When love was free,
To love her alone, alone,
  Who alone from afar loves me.'

'Why, that,' she said, 'is no reason.
  Love's always free I am told.
Will you vow to be safe from the headache
  On Tuesday, and think it will hold?'

'But you,' he replied, 'have a daughter,
    A young child, who was laid in your lap
To be pure; so I leave you:
    The angels would make me afraid.'

'Oh that,' she said, 'is no reason.
    The angels keep out of the way;
And Dora, the child, observes nothing,
    Although you should please me and stay.'

At which he rose up in his anger,—
    'Why now, you no longer are fair!
Why, now, you no longer are fatal,
    But ugly and hateful, I swear.'

At which she laughed out in her scorn:
    'These men! Oh these men overnice,
Who are shocked if a colour not virtuous
    Is frankly put on by a vice.'

Her eyes blazed upon him—'And you!
    You bring us your vices so near
That we smell them! You think in our presence
    A thought 'twould defame us to hear!

'What reason had you, and what right,—
    I appeal to your soul from my life,—
To find me so fair as a woman?
    Why, sir, I am pure, and a wife.

'Is the day-star too fair up above you?
    It burns you not. Dare you imply
I brushed you more close than the star does,
    When Walter had set me as high?

'If a man finds a woman too fair,
  He means simply adapted too much
To use unlawful and fatal. The praise!—
  Shall I thank you for such?

'Too fair?—not unless you misuse us!
  And surely if, once in a while,
You attain to it, straightaway you call us
  No longer too fair, but too vile.

'A moment,—I pray your attention!—
  I have a poor word in my head
I must utter, though womanly custom
  Would set it down better unsaid.

'You grew, sir, pale to impertinence,
  Once when I showed you a ring.
You kissed my fan when I dropped it.
  No matter! I've broken the thing.

'You did me the honour, perhaps,
  To be moved at my side now and then
In the senses—a vice, I have heard,
  Which is common to beasts and some men.

'Love's a virtue for heroes!—
  As white as the snow on high hills,
And immortal as every great soul is
  That struggles, endures, and fulfils.

'I love my Walter profoundly,—
  You, Maude, though you faltered a week,
For the sake of... what is it—an eyebrow?
  Or, less still, a mole on the cheek?

'And since, when all's said, you're too noble
    To stoop to the frivolous cant
About crimes irresistable, virtues that
    Swindle, betray and supplant.

'I determined to prove to yourself that,
    Whate'er you might dream or avow
By illusion, you wanted precisely
    No more of me than you have now.

'There! Look me full in the face!—in
    The face. Understand, if you can,
That the eyes of such women as I am
    Are clean as the palm of a man.

'Drop his hand, you insult him.
    Avoid us for fear we should cost you a scar—
You take us for harlots, I tell you,
    And not for the women we are.

'You wronged me: but then I considered…
    There's Walter! And so at the end
I vowed that he should not be mulcted,
    By me, in the hand of a friend.

'Have I hurt you indeed? We are quits then.
    Nay, friend of my Walter, be mine!
Come, Dora, my darling, my angel,
    And help me to ask him to dine.'

A MUSICAL INSTRUMENT

WHAT was he doing, the great god Pan,
    Down in the reeds by the river?
Spreading ruin and scattering ban,
Splashing and paddling with hoofs of a goat,
And breaking the golden lilies afloat
    With the dragon-fly on the river.

He tore out a reed, the great god Pan,
    From the deep cool bed of the river:
The limpid water turbidly ran,
And the broken lilies a-dying lay,
And the dragon-fly had fled away,
    Ere he brought it out of the river.

High on the shore sate the great god Pan,
    While turbidly flowed the river;
And hacked and hewed as a great god can,
With his hard bleak steel at the patient reed,
Till there was not a sign of a leaf indeed
    To prove it fresh from the river.

He cut it short, did the great god Pan,
    (How tall it stood in the river !)
Then drew the pith, like the heart of a man,
Steadily from the outside ring,
And notched the poor dry empty thing
    In holes, as he sate by the river.

'This is the way,' laughed the great god Pan,
    (Laughed while he sate by the river,)
'The only way, since gods began
To make sweet music, they could succeed.'
Then, dropping his mouth to a hole in the reed,
    He blew in power by the river.

Sweet, sweet, sweet, O Pan!
   Piercing sweet by the river!
Blinding sweet, O great god Pan!
The sun on the hill forgot to die,
And the lilies revived, and the dragon-fly
   Came back to dream on the river.

Yet half a beast is the great god Pan,
   To laugh as he sits by the river,
Making a poet out of a man:
The true gods sigh for the cost and pain,—
For the reed which grows nevermore again
   As a reed with the reeds in the river.

EXAGGERATION

WE overstate the ills of life, and take
Imagination (given us to bring down
The choirs of singing angels overshone
By God's clear glory) down our earth to rake
The dismal snows instead,—flake following flake,
To cover all the corn. We walk upon
The shadow of hills across a level thrown,
And pant like climbers. Near the alder-brake
We sigh so loud, the nightingale within
Refuses to sing loud, as else she would.
O brothers! let us leave the shame and sin
Of taking vainly, in a plaintive mood,
The holy name of Grief!—holy herein,
That by the grief of One came all our good.

THE DESERTED GARDEN

I MIND me in the days departed,
How often underneath the sun
With childish bounds I used to run
    To a garden long deserted.

The beds and walks were vanished quite;
And whereso'er had struck the spade,
The greenest grasses Nature laid,
    To sanctify her right.

I called the place my wilderness,
For no one entered there but I;
The sheep looked in, the grass to espy,
    And passed it ne' ertheless.

The trees were interwoven wild,
And spread their boughs enough about
To keep both sheep and shepherd out,
    But not a happy child.

Adventurous joy it was for me!
I crept beneath the boughs, and found
A circle smooth of mossy ground
    Beneath a poplar tree.

Old garden rose-trees hedged it in,
Bedropt with roses waxen white
Well satisfied with dew and light
    And careless to be seen.

Long years ago it might befall,
When all the garden flowers were trim,
The grave old gardener prided him
    On these the most of all.

Some lady, stately overmuch,
Here moving with a silken noise,
Has blushed beside them at the voice
   That likened her to such.

And these to make a diadem,
She often may have plucked and twined,
Half-smiling as it came to mind
   That few would look at them.

Oh, little thought that lady proud,
A child would watch her fair white rose,
When buried lay her whiter brows,
   And silk was changed for shroud!—

Nor thought that gardener (full of scorns
For men unlearned and simple phrase),
A child would bring it all its praise
   By creeping through the thorns!

To me upon my low moss seat,
Though never a dream the roses sent
Of science or love's compliment,
   I ween they smelt as sweet.

It did not move my grief to see
The trace of human step departed:
Because the garden was deserted,
   The blither place for me!

Friends blame me not! a narrow ken
Has childhood 'twixt the sun and sward:
We draw the moral afterward—
   We feel the gladness then.

And gladdest hours for me did glide
In silence at the rose-tree wall:
A thrush made gladness musical
   Upon the other side.

Nor he nor I did e'er incline
To peck or pluck the blossoms white;
How should I know but roses might
   Lead lives as glad as mine?

To make my hermit-home complete,
I brought clear water from the spring
Praised in its own low murmuring,—
   And cresses glossy wet.

And so, I thought, my likeness grew
(Without the melancholy tale)
To 'gentle hermit of the dale'.
   And Angelina too.

For oft I read within my nook
Such minstrel stories; till the breeze
Made sounds poetic in the trees,—
   And then I shut the book.

If I shut this wherein I write
I hear no more the wind athwart
Those trees,—nor feel that childish heart
   Delighting in delight.

My childhood from my life is parted,
My footstep from the moss which drew
Its fairy circle round: anew
   The garden is deserted.

Another thrush may there rehearse
The madrigals which sweetest are;
No more for me!—myself afar
   Do sing a sadder verse.

Ah me, ah me! when erst I lay
In that child's-nest so greenly wrought,
I laughed unto myself and thought
   'The time will pass away'.

And still I laughed, and did not fear
But that, whene'er was past away
The childish time, some happier play
   My womanhood would cheer.

I knew the time would pass away,
And yet, beside the rose-tree wall,
Dear God, how seldom, if at all,
   Did I look up to pray?

The time is past;—and now that grows
The cypress high among the trees,
And I behold white sepulchres
   As well as the white rose,—

When graver, meeker thoughts are given,
And I have learnt to lift my face,
Reminded how earth's greenest place
   The colour draws from heaven,—

It something saith for earthly pain,
But more for Heavenly promise free,
That I who was, would shrink to be
   That happy child again.

HUMAN LIFE'S MYSTERY

WE sow the glebe, we reap the corn,
    We build the house where we may rest,
And then, at moments, suddenly,
We look up to the great wide sky,
Inquiring wherefore we were born...
    For earnest, or for jest?

The senses folding thick and dark
    About the stifled soul within,
We guess diviner things beyond,
And yearn to them with yearning fond;
We strike out blindly to a mark
    Believed in, but not seen.

We vibrate to the pant and thrill
    Wherewith Eternity has curled
In serpent-twine about God's seat
While, freshening upward to His feet,
In gradual growth His full-leaved will
    Expands from world to world.

And in the tumult and excess
    Of act and passion under sun,
We sometimes hear—oh, soft and far,
As silver star did touch with star,
The kiss of Peace and Righteousness
    Through all things that are done.

God keeps His holy mysteries
    Just on the outside of man's dream,
In diapason slow, we think
To hear their pinions rise and sink,
While they float pure beneath His eyes,
    Like swans adown a stream.

Abstractions, are they, from the forms
    Of His great beauty? exaltations
From His great glory?—strong previsions
Of what we shall be? intuitions
Of what we are-in calms and storms,
    Beyond our peace and passions?

Things nameless! which, in passing so,
    Do stroke us with a subtle grace.
We say, 'Who passes?' —they are dumb.
We cannot see them go or come:
Their touches fall soft—cold—as snow
    Upon a blind man's face.

Yet, touching so, they draw above
    Our common thoughts to Heaven's unknown;
Our daily joy and pain, advance
To a divine significance,—
Our human love—O mortal love,
    That light is not its own!

And sometimes, horror chills our blood
    To be so near such mystic things,
And we wrap round us, for defence,
Our purple manners, moods of sense—
As angels, from the face of God,
    Stand hidden in their wings.

And sometimes, through life's heavy swound
    We grope for them!—with strangled breath
We stretch our hands abroad and try
To reach them in our agony,—
And widen, so, the broad life-wound
    Which soon is large enough for death.

INCLUSIONS

OH, wilt thou have my hand, Dear,
　　To lie along in thine?
As a little stone in a running Stream,
　　It seems to lie and pine.
Now drop the poor pale hand, Dear,...
　　Unfit to plight with thine.

Oh, wilt thou have my cheek, Dear,
　　Drawn closer to thine own?
My cheek is white, my cheek is worn,
　　By many a tear run down.
Now leave a little space, Dear,...
　　Lest it should wet thine own.

Oh, must thou have my soul, Dear,
　　Comingled with thy soul?
Red grows the cheek, and warm the hand,...
　　The part is in the whole!
Nor hands nor cheeks keep separate,
　　When soul is joined to soul.

SUBSTITUTION

WHEN some beloved voice that was to you
Both sound and sweetness, faileth suddenly,
And silence, against which you dare not cry,
Aches round you like a strong disease and new—
What hope? what help? what music will undo
That silence to your sense? Not friendship's sigh.
Not reason's subtle count. Not melody
Of viols, nor of pipes that Faunus blew.
Not songs of poets, nor of nightingales,
Whose hearts leap upward through the cypress trees

To the clear moon! nor yet the spheric laws
Self-chanted,—nor the angels' sweet All hails,
Met in the smile of God. Nay, none of these.
Speak thou, availing Christ!—and fill this pause.

DIED

WHAT shall we add now? He is dead.
   And I who praise and you who blame,
   With wash of words across his name
Find suddenly declared instead—
'On Sunday, third of August, dead.'

Which stops the whole we talked to-day.
   I, quickened to a plausive glance
   At his large general tolerance
By common people's narrow way.
Stopped short in praising. Dead, they say.

And you, who had just put in a sort
   Of cold deduction—'rather, large
   Through weakness of the continent marge,
Than greatness of the thing contained'—
Broke off. Dead!—there, you stood restrained.

As if we had talked in following one
   Up some long gallery. 'Would you choose
   An air like that? The gait is loose—
Or noble.' Sudden in the sun
An oubliette winks. Where is he? Gone.

Dead. Man's 'I was' by God's 'I am'—
   All hero-worship comes to that.
   High heart, high thought, high fame, as flat
As a gravestone. Bring your Jacet jam—
The epitaph's an epigram.

Dead. There's an answer to arrest
   All carping. Dust's his natural place!
   He'll let the flies buzz round his face
And, though you slander, not protest?
—From such an one, exact the Best?

Opinions gold or brass are null.
   We chuck our flattery or abuse,
   Called Caesar's due, as Charon's dues,
I' the teeth of some dead sage or fool,
To mend the grinning of a skull.

Be abstinent in praise and blame.
   The man's still mortal, who stands first,
   And mortal only, if last and worst.
Then slowly lift so frail a fame,
Or softly drop so poor a shame.

THE SLEEP

Of all the thoughts of God that are
Borne inward unto souls afar,
Along the Psalmist's music deep,
Now tell me if that any is,
For gift or grace, surpassing this—
'He giveth His belovèd sleep'?

What would we give to our beloved?
The hero's heart to be unmoved,
The poet's star-tuned harp, to sweep,
The patriot's voice, to teach and rouse,
The monarch's crown, to light the brows?
He giveth His belovèd, sleep.

What do we give to our beloved?
A little faith all undisproved,
A little dust to overweep,
And bitter memories to make
The whole earth blasted for our sake.
He giveth His belovèd, sleep.

'Sleep soft, beloved!' we sometimes say,
But have no tune to charm away
Sad dreams that through the eye-lids creep.
But never doleful dream again
Shall break the happy slumber when
He giveth His belovèd, sleep.

O earth, so full of dreary noises!
O men, with wailing in your voices!
O delvèd gold, the wailers heap!
O strife, O curse, that o'er it fall!
God strikes a silence through you all,
He giveth His belovèd, sleep.

His dews drop mutely on the hill;
His cloud above it saileth still,
Though on its slope men sow and reap.
More softly than the dew is shed,
Or cloud is floated overhead,
He giveth His belovèd, sleep.

Aye, men may wonder while they scan
A living, thinking, feeling man
Confirmed in such a rest to keep;
But angels say, and through the word
I think their happy smile is heard—
'He giveth His belovèd, sleep.'

For me, my heart that erst did go
Most like a tired child at a show,
That sees through tears the mummers leap,
Would now its wearied vision close,
Would child-like on His love repose,
Who giveth His belovèd, sleep.

And, friends, dear friends,—when it shall be
That this low breath is gone from me,
And round my bier ye come to weep,
Let One, most loving of you all,
Say, 'Not a tear must o'er her fall;
He giveth His belovèd, sleep.'

THE BEST THING IN THE WORLD

WHAT'S the best thing in the world?
June-rose, by May-dew impearled;
Sweet south-wind, that means no rain;
Truth, not cruel to a friend;
Pleasure, not in haste to end;
Beauty, not self-decked and curled
Till its pride is over-plain;
Light, that never makes you wink;
Memory, that gives no pain;
Love, when, *so*, you're loved again.
What's the best thing in the world?
—Something out of it, I think.

THE CHURCHYARD

To the belfry, one by one, went the ringers from the sun,
Toll slowly.
And the oldest ringer said, 'Ours is music for the Dead,
When the rebecks are all done.'

Six abeles i' the churchyard grow on the northside in a row,
Toll slowly.
And the shadows of their tops rock across the little slopes
Of the grassy graves below.

On the south side and the west, a small river runs in haste,
Toll slowly.
And between the river flowing and the fair green trees
agrowing
Do the dead lie at their rest.

In your patience ye are strong; cold and heat ye take not wrong.
Toll slowly.
When the trumpet of the angel blows eternity's evangel,
Time will seem to you not long.

Oh, the little birds sang east, and the little birds sang west,
Toll slowly.
And I said in underbreath,—All our life is mixed with death,
And who knoweth which is best?

Oh, the little birds sang east, and the little birds sang west,
Toll slowly.
And I smiled to think God's greatness flowed around our
incompleteness,—
Round our restlessness, His rest.

From *The Rime of the Duchess May*

MY DOVES

MY little doves have left a nest
   Upon an Indian tree,
Whose leaves fantastic take their rest
   Or motion from the sea;
For, ever there, the sea-winds go
With sunlit paces to and fro.

The tropic flowers looked up to it,
   The tropic stars looked down,
And there my little doves did sit,
   With feathers softly brown,
And glittering eyes that showed their right
To general Nature's deep delight.

And God them taught, at every close
   Of murmuring waves beyond,
And green leaves round, to interpose
   Their choral voices fond,
Interpreting that love must be
The meaning of the earth and sea.

Fit ministers! Of living loves,
   Theirs bath the calmest fashion,
Their living voice the likest moves
   To lifeless intonation.
The lovely monotone of springs
And winds, and such insensate things.

My little doves were ta'en away
   From that glad nest of theirs,
Across an ocean rolling grey,
   And tempest-clouded airs:
My little doves,—who lately knew
The sky and wave by warmth and blue!

And now, within the city prison,
    In mist and chillness pent,
With sudden upward look they listen
    For sounds of past content!—
For lapse of water, swell of breeze,
Or nut-fruit falling from the trees.

The star without the glow of passion,
    The triumph of the mart,
The gold and silver as they clash on
    Man's cold metallic heart—
The roar of wheels, the cry for bread,—
These only sounds are heard instead.

Yet still, as on my human hand
    Their fearless heads they lean,
And almost seem to understand
    What human musings mean,
(Their eyes, with such a plaintive shine,
Are fastened upwardly to mine!)

Soft falls their chant as on the nest
    Beneath the sunny zone;
For love that stirred it in their breast
    Has not aweary grown,
And 'neath the city's shade can keep
The well of music clear and deep.

And love that keeps the music, fills
    With pastoral memories:
All echoings from out the hills,
    All droppings from the skies,
All flowings from the wave and wind,
Remembered in their chant, I find.

So teach ye me the wisest part.
    My little doves! to move
Along the city-ways with heart
    Assured by holy love,
And vocal with such songs as own
A fountain to the world unknown.

'Twas hard to sing by Babel's stream—
    More hard, in Babel's street!
But if the soulless creatures deem
    Their music not unmeet
For sunless walls—let us begin,
Who wear immortal wings within!

To me, fair memories belong,
    Of scenes that used to bless,
For no regret, but present song,
    And lasting thankfulness,
And very soon to break away,
Like types, in purer things than they.

I will have hopes that cannot fade,
    For flowers the valley yields!
I will have humble thoughts instead
    Of silent, dewy fields!
My spirit and my God shall be
My seaward hill, my boundless sea.